C000291760

Experiments In Growing Potatoes...

Charles Sumner Plumb

Nabu Public Domain Reprints:

You are holding a reproduction of an original work published before 1923 that is in the public domain in the United States of America, and possibly other countries. You may freely copy and distribute this work as no entity (individual or corporate) has a copyright on the body of the work. This book may contain prior copyright references, and library stamps (as most of these works were scanned from library copies). These have been scanned and retained as part of the historical artifact.

This book may have occasional imperfections such as missing or blurred pages, poor pictures, errant marks, etc. that were either part of the original artifact, or were introduced by the scanning process. We believe this work is culturally important, and despite the imperfections, have elected to bring it back into print as part of our continuing commitment to the preservation of printed works worldwide. We appreciate your understanding of the imperfections in the preservation process, and hope you enjoy this valuable book.

NOMY LABORATORY

no. 8

BULLETIN _No. 8_

OF THE

AGRICULTURAL EXPERIMENT STATION,

OF THE

UNIVERSITY OF TENNESSEE,

STATE AGRICULTURAL and MECHANICAL COLLEGE.

Vol. III.	JANUARY, 1890.	No. 1.

EXPERIMENTS IN GROWING POTATOES.

These Bulletins are sent, free of charge, to farmers who apply to the
Experiment Station,

KNOXVILLE, TENNESSEE,

U. S. A.

THE AGRICULTURAL EXPERIMENT STATION

OF THE UNIVERSITY OF TENNESSEE.

BOARD OF CONTROL:

O. P. TEMPLE.   R. H. ARMSTRONG.

JAMES PARK, D.D.   J. W. GAUT.

TREASURER:

JAMES COMFORT.

THE STATION COUNCIL IS COMPOSED OF ITS OFFICERS:

CHARLES W. DABNEY, Jr. Ph. D., Director.

CHAS. S. PLUMB, B.S., Assistant Director.

F. L. SCRIBNER, Botanist.

H. E. SUMMERS, B.S., Entomologist.

L. P. BROWN, Acting Chemist.

R. J. CUMMINGS, Farm Foreman.

W. N. PRICE, Assistant.

The Station has good facilities for analyzing and testing fertilizers, cattle foods, milk and dairy products; seeds, with reference to their purity or germinating power; for identifying grasses and weeds and studying forage plants; for investigating the diseases of fruits and fruit trees, grains and other useful plants; for making reports on injurious insects, and the best means of combatting them.

The Bulletins and Reports will be sent, free of charge, to all farmers.

Packages by express, to receive attention, should be *prepaid*.

All communications should be addressed, *not to any individual officer*, but simply to the

EXPERIMENT STATION,

KNOXVILLE, TENN.

☞ The Experiment Station building, containing its offices, laboratories and museum, and the plant-house and horticultural department are located on the University grounds, fifteen minutes walk from the Custom House in Knoxville. The Experiment Farm stables, milk laboratory, etc., are located one mile west of the University on the Kingston pike. The farmers are especially invited to visit the buildings and experimental grounds.

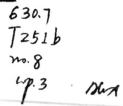

630.7
T251b
no. 8
cp. 3

DIVISION OF FIELD AND FEEDING EXPERIMENTS.

Experiments in Growing Potatoes.

BY C. S. PLUMB.

The experiments conducted by this Division with the potato during 1889, may be classified and discussed under the following headings:

(a) **Concerning the Influence of the Amount of Seed Tuber Planted upon the Resulting Crop of Irish Potatoes.**

(b) **Trial of the Rural New Yorker Trench System of Potato Culture.**

(c) **Tests of Varieties of Irish Potatoes.**

(d) **Early vs. Late Culture for Sweet Potatoes.**

In all the above experiments the potatoes were grown on a clay-loam soil, with a heavy clay sub-soil. The plats were quite level, and the conditions normal during the growth of the plants. Before digging, when the plants were about ripe, very frequent rains caused a vigorous growth of weeds, which interfered with harvesting. The ground, however, was kept well tilled up to a point where weed growth could not injure the crop yield.

(a) Concerning the Influence of the Amount of Seed Tuber Planted upon the Resulting Crop.

Many experiments have been conducted for comparing the productiveness of large, medium and small whole tubers, half and quarter tubers, and single eyes. However, in such comparisons the size of tuber has been one of approximation ; in other words, a large tuber might mean quite a different size or weight, at one station from that at another.

(I.) *Comparing whole tubers of different weights for seed.* In order to get more complete information on the relation of the tuber planted to the resulting crop, the following experiments were carried out:

Eight different lots of whole tubers of Early Rose potatoes, were selected; each lot, with one exception, consisting of 100 tubers. Every potato in each group was weighed on a Fairbank's silk scale, in order to insure accuracy. Each lot was planted in a row by itself, the rows being three and one-half feet apart, and the tubers were two feet apart in the row, with the exception of row 1, in which they were three feet apart. The ground had the best of tillage, but no fertilizers were used. Planting was done on the trench system, on April 6th, and hoeing and cultivating occurred whenever necessary. Table I. gives the figures of interest up to harvesting:

TABLE I.

Row	Weight of Tubers	No. Tubers Planted	Date of Vegetation	No. Tubers Vegetated	Bloomed	Height of Plants June 20	Ripe
1	12 to 14 ozs	46	April 24	46	May 22	20 inch	July 10
2	10 " 12 "	100	" 24	100	" 25	20 "	" 10
3	8 " 10 "	100	" 22	100	" 25	17 "	" 8
4	6 " 8 "	100	" 22	100	" 25	17 "	" 4
5	4 " 6 "	100	" 22	100	" 25	16½ "	" 4
6	3 " 4 "	100	" 22	100	" 27	15½ "	" 5
7	2 " 3 "	100	" 24	100	" 27	16½ "	" 8
8	1 " 2 "	100	" 24	100	" 27	15 "	" 9

These facts appear evident upon an examination of the above figures:

(1) The *largest* tubers bloomed first, produced the highest (and also largest) growth of plants.

(2) The *smallest* tubers bloomed last, produced the lowest (and smallest) plants, and ripened one day earlier than the largest.

(3) *Large size* apparently favored earliness of bloom, height and size of plant, and, to a certain extent, delayed ripening.

(4) Plants from tubers weighing from four to eight ounces ripened earlier than those from tubers of greater or lesser weights.

At harvesting, the potatoes in each hill in the several lots were dug, and, after being cleaned, weighed and counted, the tubers being separated into merchantable and unmerchantable, anything as large or above an average hen's egg in size being rated as merchantable. The few rotten ones were classed as unmerchantable. The figures resulting from this harvest number several thousands, consequently only those of special interest are presented in Tables II. and III.

TABLE II.
YIELD OF 100 TUBERS, EACH IN DIFFERENT ROWS.

Weight of Each Tuber Planted,	MERCHANTABLE.		UNMERCHANTABLE.		TOTAL CROP.	
	Weight.	Number Tubers.	Weight.	Number Tubers.	Weight.	Number Tubers.
12 to 14 ozs.	46 lbs.	269	39 lbs. 15 ozs	621	85 lbs. 15 ozs.	890
10 " 12 "	95 " 14 ozs	584	94 " 12 "	1369	190 " 10 "	1953
8 " 10 "	102 " 12 "	623	63 " 3 "	1049	165 " 15 "	1672
6 " 8 "	80 " 6 "	511	62 " 6 "	1123	142 " 12 "	1634
4 " 6 "	74 " 5 "	519	59 " 15 "	1022	134 " 4 "	1541
3 " 4 "	66 " 13 "	475	56 " 15 "	1008	123 " 12 "	1483
2 " 3 "	72 " 11 "	469	46 " 12 "	690	119 " 7 "	1159
1 " 2 "	62 " 1 "	363	45 " 12 "	584	107 " 13 "	947

* 46 hills planted.

Table II shows the yield of each lot of tubers, but as each group was not planted with equal numbers of potatoes, a comparison by yield per hill is the only fair way to note the relative results. This comparative yield is presented in Table III., the figures being in ounces and fractions.

TABLE III.
AVERAGE YIELD PER HILL OF POTATOES IN DIFFERENT LOTS.

Weight of Tubers Planted	MERCHANTABLE.		UNMERCHANTABLE.		TOTAL CROP.	
	Weight.	Number Tubers.	Weight	Number Tubers	Weight	Number Tubers
12 to 14 ozs.	16.	5.8	13.8	13.5	**29.8**	**19.3**
10 " 12 "	15.	5.7	14.8	13.4	**29.9**	**19.1**
8 " 10 "	16.4	6.2	10.1	10.4	**26.5**	**16.7**
6 " 8 "	12.8	5.1	9.9	11.2	**22.8**	**16.3**
4 " 6 "	11.8	5.1	9.5	10.2	**21.4**	**15.4**
3 " 4 "	10.6	4.7	9.1	10.	**19.8**	**14.8**
2 " 3 "	11.6	4.6	7.4	6.9	**19.1**	**11.5**
1 " 2 "	10.	3.6	7.3	5.8	**17.4**	**9.5**

It will be noted in Table III. that, with very slight variation, the **productiveness per hill was greatest with the largest planted tubers; and** in the case of the total crop, **decreased quite constantly with decrease of weight of seed planted.** This relationship of weight of tuber planted to weight of yield per hill, is graphically and fairly shown in the following eight vertical lines. The figures at the base of the lines, indicate the weight of seed used

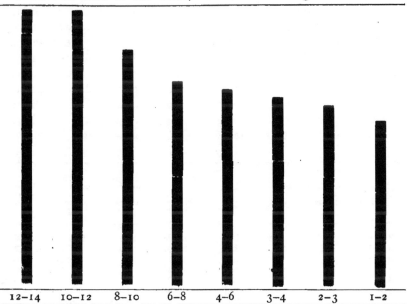

| 12–14 | 10–12 | 8–10 | 6–8 | 4–6 | 3–4 | 2–3 | 1–2 |

DIAGRAM SHOWING THE RELATION OF SIZE OF TUBER PLANTED TO CROP YIELD.

An ordinary glance at the preceding tables, would indicate that the farmer, to get the largest crop of potatoes, should use large rather than small seed tubers. However, there are several questions of importance bearing on the profit or loss of using whole tubers for seed. These may be discussed as follows.

(1) The amount of potatoes per acre to be used as seed. Planted as these were in the experiment, 4,714 of the 12 to 14 oz. tubers would occupy one acre of land, and 7,072 tubers of the other weight, would occupy the same space. According to this, we find that 3,830 lbs., or 64 bu. of 12 to 14 oz. potatoes would plant one acre.

4,862 "	" 81 "	" 10 to 12 "	"	"	"	"	"
3,978 "	" 66 "	" 8 to 10 "	"	"	"	"	"
3,094 "	" 52 "	" 6 to 8 "	"	"	"	"	"
2,210 "	" 37 "	" 4 to 6 "	"	"	"	"	"
1,547 "	" 26 "	" 3 to 4 "	"	"	"	"	"
1,105 "	" 18 "	" 2 to 3 "	"	"	"	"	"
663 "	" 11 "	" 1 to 2 "	"	"	"	"	"

In the case of large seed, a considerable expense would be necessary to either grow or purchase tubers for extensive planting, for it will require as much as 81 bushels of 10 to 12 oz. tubers to plant an acre, against 11 bushels of 1 to 2 oz. tubers, a saving of 70 bushels per acre of seed. And here question two arises.

(2) What is the relation of cost of seed to return in crop? This is seen in Table IV., which gives the yield per acre, in weight and number of tubers, cost of seed per acre, value of crop per acre and shows the balance in favor of the crop. In examining this table, it is to be distinctly remembered that it is simply comparative. The total potato crop only is considered and all items of expense aside from cost of seed are left out, as they are practically the same. As the relation of merchantable to unmerchantable tubers is quite alike in each lot, I have classed all the potatoes at 40 cents per bushel, as an average sale price. So also the price of seed is made the same, whether large or small. Yet if the sale price is reduced to an average of 20 or 30 cents, it will not in any way injure the value of the figures. The table is as follows:

TABLE IV.

Weight of Each Seed and Distance Planted Apart.	Yield.		Cost of Seed per Acre, at 75 c. per Bushel.	Value of Crop per Acre, at 40c. per Bushel.	Balance in Favor of Crop.
	Bushels.	Number Tubers.			
12 – 14 ozs., 3 feet apart	146	90,980	$48 00	$58 40	$10 40
10 – 12 " 2 " "	220	135,075	60 75	88 00	17 25
8 – 10 " " " "	195	118,102	49 50	78 00	28 50
6 – 8 " " " "	168	115,273	39 00	67 20	28 20
4 – 6 " " " "	158	108,908	27 75	63 20	35 45
3 – 4 " " " "	146	104,665	19 50	58 40	38 90
2 – 3 " " " "	141	81,328	13 50	56 40	42 90
1 – 2 " " " "	128	67,184	8 25	51 20	42 95

An examination of this table, suggests a third and most important question, viz.:

(3) What is the relation of yield to profit on crop? The larger the tuber planted, the smaller the profit, and the smaller the tuber planted, the larger the profit, and with the exception of a difference of thirty cents in favor of 8 to 10 oz. tubers over 6 to 8 oz., this relationship is very striking.*

As bearing directly on the above experiments, additional data may be brought to the reader's attention at this point, as the result of other tests with different quantities of seed or methods of cutting

(II.) *Comparing large and medium sized whole tubers, and halves, quarters and single eyes.* Six plats, of one-fourth acre each, were used in this experiment. The plats were 272 feet long, and contained 13 rows each, the rows being three and one-half feet apart. No fertilizer was used, but the land was well cultivated and worked after plowing. Early Rose, northern grown, seed potatoes were used.

TABLE V.

QUARTER-ACRE POTATO PLATS.

No. of Plat	Size of Seed	Planted	Vege-tated.	Bu. Sd. planted in Plat.	No. Sd. Potat's planted	No. Sd. Potat's Vegt'd	Bloomed	Height Plants June 20	Ripe
I.	Large	Mar. 22	Apr. 8	18½	2373	2294	May 12	22½in	July 15
II.	Medium........	" 22	" 13	14½	3536	3469	" 13	16½ "	" 15
III.	" halves...	" 23	" 13	10	3536	3482	" 21	11¾ "	" 15
IV.	" quarters.	" 23	" 13	5	3536	3506	" 20	18 "	" 15
V.	Lar. single eyes	" 22	" 13	3½	3536	3390	" 15	17¼ "	" 17
VI.	Med. " "	" 22	" 13	2¾	3536	3431	" 19	15½ "	" 17

From Table V. we see that the large whole seed produced the highest plants, but this is the only feature of growth in which the large seed differs from the small.

The results in yield are clearly shown in Table VI. In digging the crop, the same selection was made as in the preceding experiments. The figures given are only totals and averages of the 13 rows in each plat.

* That the reader may have a clearer idea of the relative sizes of the potatoes planted, I give the following figures in inches of the extreme length, breadth and thickness of fair samples of Early Rose potatoes such as we planted. These figures are from actual measurements;

12 to 14 ounce Early Rose potatoes measure about	6	x3	x2	inches.
10 to 12	"	"	"	"	"	"	5	x2¾x2¼	"
8 to 10	"	"	"	"	"	"	5	x2½x2	"
6 to 8	"	"	"	"	"	"	3½x2½x2¼	"
4 to 6	"	"	"	"	"	"	3½x2 x1½	"
3 to 4	"	"	"	"	"	"	2¾x2 x1½	"
2 to 3	"	"	"	"	"	"	2½x2 x1½	"
1 to 2	"	"	"	"	"	"	2¼x1½x1¼	"

TABLE VI
Yield in Pounds.

Plat.	MERCHANTABLE.		UNMERCHANTABLE		TOTAL CROP.		Cost of Seed at 75c. per Bushel. Per Acre	VALUE of Crop at 40c. per Bushel. Per Acre	VALUE of Crop over cost of Seed. Per Acre
	Weight.	Number.	Weight.	Number.	Weight.	Number.			
I.	2536	13,050	1373½	23,352	3909½	36,402	$55 50	$104 00	$48 50
II.	1737½	9,923	1207	19,814	2944½	29,737	43 50	78 40	34 90
III.	1091½	7,740	1243	23,815	2334½	31,555	30 00	62 40	32 40
IV.	1456	7,477	985	14,113	2441	21,590	15 00	64 80	49 80
V.	1255	5,664	667	7,952	1922	13,616	10 50	51 20	40 70
VI.	830	3,662	691½	7,497	1521½	11,159	8 24	40 40	32 16

We learn from this table two important facts: (1) Whole large tubers produced a larger crop and greater value over cost of seed than did the medium sized tubers. (2) Single eyes from large tubers gave a larger and more valuable crop than single eyes from medium sized tubers.

It will be noted that plat IV. yielded a larger crop than plat III. by over 100 pounds. Yet from the results preceding, and those following, it will be seen that the general weight of testimony would indicate that the reverse result is to be expected.

Another experiment bearing on this same question of quantity of seed tubers to be used, was conducted, and is reported as a third comparison.

(III.) *Comparing whole tubers with halves from wholes of the same weight.*

This experiment had two objects. (a) To note the difference in yield between a certain number of tubers of the same size, planted whole, and twice that number of halves from potatoes of the same size as the wholes. (b) To note if the eyes on the under side of a whole potato, materially increase the yield over the half potato, planted with the eyes facing outward or upward.

Five hundred and forty Early Rose potatoes, each of which weighed six to seven ounces, were divided into two lots of 270 each. Lot I., the wholes, was planted in three rows, there being 90 tubers to the row, each being 18 inches apart in the row, and the rows three and one-half feet apart. Lot II. thus contained 540 half tubers. As arranged, Lot II. contained the same weight of potato, and number of eyes, as did Lot I. Both lots were planted alike, and each received the same treatment. Lot II. occupied six rows, and the halves were placed with the cut side under. No fertilizer was used. All of the plats vegetated and bloomed at the same time. In five out of the nine rows, a very few hills produced no potatoes. Table VII., which contains the yields, brings out the comparative difference sought for. Since the complete tables contain nearly 5,000 weights and numbers, as in the preceding cases, only totals and averages of the whole are given.

TABLE VII.

COMPARATIVE YIELDS OF WHOLE VS. HALF POTATOES.

No. of Row	No. of Hills	MERCHANTABLE				UNMERCHANTABLE				TOTAL CROP.			
		Weight		Number		Weight		Number		Weight		Number	
		Total	Avrge. per Hill	Total	Avrge. per Hill	Total	Avrge. per Hill	Total	Avrge. per Hill	Total	Avrge. per Hill	Total	Avrge. per Hill
1	90	48.7	8.6	303	3.3	62.8	11.1	983	10.9	110.15	19.7	1286	14.2
2	90	46.14	9.3	290	3.2	52.15	9.4	874	9.3	99.13	17.7	1164	12.9
3	84	46.4	8.8	273	3.2	61.4	11.6	978	11.6	107.8	20.4	1251	14.8
Lot I. — Total Wt. for 270 wholes		141.9	25.7	866	9.7	176.11	32.1	2835	31.5	318.4	57.8	3701	41.9
Average per hill of 270 wholes			**8.5**		**3.2**		**10.7**		**10.5**		**19.5**		**13.9**
1	89	49.8	8.8	265	2.9	41.13	7.5	556	6.2	91.5	16.4	821	9.2
2	88	57.2	10.3	293	3.3	37.2	6.7	541	6.1	94.4	17.1	834	9.4
3	87	58.6	10.7	321	3.6	29.10	5.4	438	5.	88.	16.1	759	8.7
4	84	61.4	11.6	362	4.3	27.4	5.1	451	5.3	88.8	16.8	813	9.6
5	90	55.	9.7	353	3.9	31.14	5.6	534	5.9	86.14	15.4	887	9.8
6	90	59.6	10.5	356	3.9	28.12	5.1	492	5.4	88.2	15.6	848	9.4
Lot II. — Total Wt. for 540 halves		340.10	61.6	1950	21.9	196.7	35.4	3012	33.9	537.1	97.4	4962	56.1
Average per hill of 540 halves			**10.3**		**3.6**		**5.9**		**5.6**		**16.4**		**9.3**

Table VII. is interesting as demonstrating, as far as this experiment goes, the following facts. These are clearly shown in the heavy black figures in the table.

(a) The *half tubers* produced a greater number and greater weight of merchantable potatoes, *per hill*, than did the whole tubers

(b) The *whole tubers* produced very nearly twice as many unmerchantable tubers, *per hill*, as did the half tubers.

(*c*) The average weight of one hill grown from a whole tuber was 19.5 ozs., while that from half tubers was 16.4 ozs., or an increase per hill of 8.4 per cent. by using whole tubers for seed.

(*d*) The size of the potatoes grown with half seed is somewhat larger than those from whole seed.

Summary of above Experiments.

(1) The larger the potato planted, the larger the plant produced, and the more abundant the harvest in tubers.

(2) Other things being equal, the fewer the number of eyes in a piece of seed potato, or the smaller that piece of seed, the smaller the crop that will be produced.

(3) The larger the quantity of whole tuber placed in a hill for seed, the greater the cost per acre of planting, and the smaller the profit on the crop.

(4) Large and whole tubers produced smaller and poorer merchantable ones, than did half or quarter tubers, or single eyes.

(5) Large and whole tubers yielded appreciably more small, unmerchantable potatoes, than did parts of medium tubers or single eyes.

(6) Given, two potatoes of equal size, one planted whole will not yield so large nor so good a crop as will the other tuber cut into halves and each part planted in a separate hill.

(7) Referring to the point III. (*b*) on page 9, the investigation, as carried out, suggests that, in view of the fact that the whole tuber produced comparatively more small, inferior potatoes than did the halves planted, the source of these inferior tubers may be from those eyes located on the under side of the whole potato planted. This because the eyes and shoots thus located are repressed in growth to a certain extent, owing to the pressure upon them and reversal of position.

It is to be remembered that the above conclusions are the result of the investigations recorded and are based on nothing else. Neither in farm practice nor experimental work do we consider that they will *always* find endorsement. Yet as the result of much experimental work with seed potatoes, it is confidently believed that these conclusions will generally be fairly accurate.

(b) Trial of the Rural New Yorker Trench System of Potato Culture.

The following experiment was attempted on a practical basis to test the flat culture system advocated for some years by Mr. E. S.

Carman, editor of the *Rural New Yorker*. The simple object in view was, to see how large a crop of potatoes could be grown on a measured acre of ground, and to get such facts as would determine its adaptability and economy to this region. Mr. Carman has succeeded in growing some large crops. The advantages of the system, as claimed by him are, that the potato suffers from sun-burn and drought when elevated in a ridge or hill, as it does not when planted in a trench; that it is easier to cultivate *down* about the stem of the plant, than *up* against it; that moisture and fertilizers are more readily and evenly distributed about in the soil when the surface of the ground is not covered by hillocks; and that general cultivation is much easier when the plants grow on a level with the surface.

In this practical experiment, an attempt has been made to follow out the method of Mr. Carman as he has described it in the *Rural New Yorker*. The facts are as follows:

On a fairly level surface of clay-loam soil, one acre was surveyed off with instruments. The land had had clover growing upon it for three years previous. After being thoroughly plowed to a depth of about eight inches, it was well cultivated with a disk harrow, and then followed by a Thomas smoothing harrow. Then every three feet apart, trenches eight inches in depth were plowed across the field from east to west.

At the time of planting, 500 pounds of National Vegetable Grower, a good potato fertilizer, were evenly distributed along the bottom of all the furrows. Over this was dragged with hoes, about one inch of soil.

Early Rose potatoes were used for seed, a two-eye piece being placed every foot in the row. These pieces were covered with about an inch of soil, and then another quarter ton of fertilizer evenly distributed in the furrows. The trenches were then filled with soil about even with the surface. On April 29th, when the plants were about two inches high, 1000 pounds of Vegetable Grower were spread broadcast over the field and cultivated in.

Planting was done March 30th and April 3rd. The plants vegetated April 16th, bloomed May 25th, and were ripe July 17th. The field was hoed once, and cultivated three times. The culture was as nearly level as possible at all times. Owing to almost daily showers the acre was not dug till August 22–26.

The account kept of this experiment is as follows:

	Dr.	Cr.
By 1 ton National Vegetable Grower		$30 00
" 13 bushels seed potatoes, @ 80c. per bushel..........		10 40
" 31 days labor, @ $1.00 per day		31 00
" 3 days horse labor, @ $2.00 per day.............		6 00
To 94½ bushels merchantable potatoes, @ 40c. per bushel	$37 80	
" 94 " unmerchantable (small) " 15c. "	14 10	
	$51 90	$77 40
To balance......	25 50	
	$77 40	$77 40

It is unnecessary to add any other figures, such as interest or use of land, tools, etc. As the reader can see, the cost of labor and fertilizers surpassed the income from the yield of 188½ bushels of potatoes.

The cause of the comparatively small yield is not apparent. The plants made a generous and healthy growth, and so thoroughly covered the ground that a large crop was anticipated. The lack of yield is not ascribed to the system of culture. The only explanation suggested is that the fertilizer was not readily enough available to the plants, as in digging it was found in places quite unchanged.

We have detailed this work hoping that the general method of culture adopted may receive some practical attention from farmers who may read this Bulletin It is noteworthy that over 700 bushels of potatoes were raised on slightly less than a measured acre of land. in Maine, by this trench system of culture, during the season of 1889.

(c) Tests of Varieties.

Seventy-five varieties of potatoes were tested, the yields from whole tubers, halves, quarters and single eyes being recorded. The varieties were all planted under equal conditions, excepting in size of seed. As the samples were received from various seedsmen, some were larger than others, though as a rule the potatoes were of medium size. The ground they were planted in was a clay loam that received no fertilizer. Each variety was placed one foot apart in a row, and the length of the row depended upon the number of hills planted. The figures given in the following table are all average ones. That is, if, for example, 15 single-eye hills produced 150 ounces of potatoes, one hill averaged 10 ounces.

Following this table are notes concerning the varieties, such as may be of service or interest to the potato grower.

TABLE VIII.

Variety Yields: Average of Total Crop.

No.	Name of Variety.	Source of Seed.	Weight per hill in ounces				Number per hill of Tubers			
			Whole Tuber	Half Tuber	Quarter Tuber	Single Eye	Whole	Half	Quarter	Single Eye
1	American Giant	Everitt	16.6	...	...		13.9	...	...	...
2	Beauty of Hebron	{Henderson / Landreth	...		21.7	8.2	...		12.6	5 3
3	Bliss's Triumph	Everitt	29.0				12.2			
4	Boley's Northern Spy	Wilson	..	...	...	18.6	...	...	...	4.6
5	Boston Market	Vick	20.2	...	11.5	9.4	15.4		6 0	4.6
6	Burbank	{Johnson & Co. / Landreth	..	...	26.5	17.0	...		6.7	3.6
7	California Peach Blow	Everitt	24 8	...	...		15 2			
8	Charles Downing	{Henderson / Landreth				11.1	...			6.1
9	Charter Oak	Henderson	.			13.7				6.9
10	Chicago Market	Vick	20.0	...	18.6	14.4	5.4		8.5	6.5
11	Clark's No. 1	{Henderson / Thorburn	54.0	..	19.0	8.0	18.0		12.5	4.0
12	Crown Queen	Everitt	16.9				13.3			..
13	Dakota Red	{Thorburn / Everitt	4.0	..	32.2	24.6	3.0		7.5	4.9
14	Dakota Seedling	Everitt	5.9				3.1			
15	Dictator	Thorburn			30.0	22 4			8.0	4.8
16	Early Albino	Thorburn			6.5	7.4			5.7	5.5
17	Early Gem	Vick	19 1		13.2	6.8	14.0		9.2	3.7
18	Early Goodrich	Johnson & Co.			13.0	4.8			6.5	3.0
19	Early Market	Vick	19 4		11 2	7.3	5.6		4.2	2.0
20	Early Ohio	{Henderson / Vick	20.4	17.0	13.0	3.8	7.8	3.5	6.0	2.6
21	Early Rose	{Henderson / Johnson				8.6	...			4.5
22	Early Sunrise	{Henderson / Thorburn / Bouk	43.0		10.5	5.7	24.0		8.5	3.6
23	Early Puritan	{Henderson / Thorburn	45.7		19.2	3.9	29.0	..	13.7	3.7
24	Early Vermont	Landreth	29.7		8.0	5.6	24.0		5.2	3.0
25	Empire State	Henderson				17.9				4.2
26	Garfield	Landreth	43 7		9.0		12.0		5.2	
27	Everitt	Everitt	28.1				15.0			
28	Gen. McLean	Wilson			25.5	12.8			14.7	3.1
29	Great Eastern	Thorburn			28.5	16.0			15.7	5.0
30	Green Mountain	{Vick / Wilson / Everitt	11.8	23 5	13.7	20.0	4.9	6.5	5.5	5.8
31	Illinois	Everitt	16.0				8.3	...		...
32	June Early	{Wilson / Everitt	35.3			9.2	16.4			4.4
33	Late Beauty of Hebron	Thorburn			7.0	19.0			13.0	6.2
34	Maine Rose	Wilson				17.9				5.2
35	Mammoth Pearl	Landreth	57.0		19.5	7.0	29.0		8.7	4.8
36	Mammoth White Chief	Bouk			..	3.6				1.1
37	Mayflower	Landreth			15.2	9.7			10.7	6.0
38	McFadden's Favorite	Bouk				12.8				3.5
39	Morning Star	Landreth	.		45.2	21.8			11.7	4.6

TABLE VIII.—*Continued.*

Variety Yields: Average of Total Crops.

No.	Name of Variety.	Source of Seed.	Weight per hill in ounces.				Number per hill of Tubers			
			Whole Tuber	Half Tuber	Quarter Tuber	Single Eye	Whole	Half	Quarter	Single Eye
40	New Queen	{ Everitt / Bouk	25.8			10.2	12.0			5.0
41	North Georgia (Native) ..	Johnson & Co.	41.0	17.5	20.5	19.9	23.0	17.5	11.7	5.9
42	No. 50 Seedling	Vick	45.0	24.0	18.0	14.3	24.0	26.0	13.2	5.8
43	Ohio Junior	Vick	24.2	19.5	13.2	4.7	8.3	7.5	5.5	2.7
44	O. K. Mammoth Prolific..	Thorburn			34.7	20.3			13.5	5.6
45	Peach Blow Seedling	Bouk				4.6				1.5
46	Pearl of Savoy	{ Henderson / Thorburn			4.0	13.0			4.0	7.6
47	Peerless	Johnson & Co.	43.0		27.5	13.2	24.0		10.2	4.9
48	Perfect Peach Blow	{ Henderson / Vick	7.8		9.5	21.3	3.4		4.0	9.7
49	Poland	Everitt	22.3				15.6			
50	Potentate	Everitt	22.5				11.2			
51	Prairie Queen	Bouk				4.7				2.3
52	Pride of Nebraska	Bouk				5.2				2.1
53	Pride of the Field	Wilson				16.1				4.2
54	Prince Ed. Island Rose...	Landreth	34.0	10.2	11.7	6.3	31.0	7.5	6.2	4.4
55	Rose's Beauty of Beauties	Bouk				2.5				1.4
56	Rose's Beauty of Hebron.	{ Thorburn / Vick	22.0		33.0	21.0	13.0		13.0	6.4
57	Rose's New Giant	Thorburn			28.5	17.3			11.2	3.3
58	Rose's Seedling	Wilson				20.1				4.3
59	Rural Blush	{ Henderson / Thorburn			14.5	16.0			4.2	4.5
60	Rural New Yorker No. 2.	{ Henderson / Thorburn			17.5	14.9			8.5	4.0
61	Snowflake	Johnson & Co.	72.0	28.5	19.7	13.2	16.0	15.5	11.0	4.0
62	Snow Queen	Thorburn			15.5	8.0			6.2	5.1
63	State of Maine	{ Landreth / Wilson	50.5		24.5	21.6	15.0		9.2	4.7
64	Stray Beauty	Wilson				5.4				2.2
65	Sunlit Star	Wilson			19.2	11.5			13.7	6.2
66	Triumph	Henderson				5.5				4.0
67	Thorburn	Thorburn			10.5	7.4			10.5	5.5
68	Thorburn's Late Rose....	Wilson			32.0	25.4			21.2	6.8
69	Vanguard	Henderson				5.5				5.0
70	Vick's Prize	Vick	17.4	45.5	11.0	8.0	11.9	17.0	4.0	3.4
71	Watson's Seedling	Wilson				18.8				8.1
72	White Elephant	{ Thorburn / Johnson & Co.	47.0		37.1	15.8	15.0		7.7	4.1
73	White Star.	{ Henderson / Johnson / Vick	18.5	27.2	14.0	7.7	5.5	6.2	3.8	2.0
74	White Superior	Vick	20.6		16.0	15.0	8.1		4.0	3.6
	Average Yield per Hill		29.0	23.6	18.8	12.2	15.0	11.9	8.9	4.5

I would especially direct the reader's attention to the relationship of size of seed tuber to crop production. While in each class of plantings the yield is variable often to a considerable extent, an average of all the hills in each class of seed planted of 74 varieties, shows a continual decrease in yield and number of tubers per hill, from the whole potato down to the single eye. In brief, **the experiments at this Station on the relation of size of seed tubers to crop yield, demonstrate that the larger the piece of seed potato planted, the greater will be the yield.** This, it may be said, is also the result very generally arrived at, at other stations that have done similar work

VARIETY NOTES.*

American Giant (Everitt). A large, strong grower, of deep green foliage. Tuber large, long, sometimes prongy, white. Skin rather smooth, eyes few and shallow; often more than twice as long as broad. A desirable potato.

Beauty of Hebron (Henderson). A small, weakly grower, producing small, insignificant tubers. Form roundish to oblong; white, rather rough skinned; eyes shallow and few. Seed from Landreth produced a larger and longer tuber than the above, that made a fair showing.

Bliss's Triumph (Everitt). A rank, luxurious grower, producing round, rough, red skinned, deep eyed tuber. Size of tuber fair, even, rarely prongy. Worthy of further trial.

Boley's Northern Spy (Wilson). Vigorous grower, healthy, dark green. Tuber white, smooth skinned, deep eyed, long, broad, regular in size and shape. Makes a fine showing.

Boston Market (Vick). A fair grower. Form of tuber very irregular A white potato of pinkish cast in some cases, somewhat long and slender, skin rough, eyes not prominent.

Burbank (Johnson). A large, strong grower, that makes a good showing. Tuber white, oblong, smooth, eyes not prominent. A desirable potato.

California Peachblow (Everitt) Growth large, vigorous, dark green. Tubers flattish, oblong, white, with fairly smooth skin, shallow eyes; uneven in size.

Charles Downing (Thorburn). Plant growth very inferior. Tuber abruptly oblong or round, rough white skin, eyes prominent. Makes a poor showing all around.

Charter Oak (Henderson). Tuber oblong, white, less than twice as long as broad, rather rough skin, eyes shallow and few. Not desirable.

*The name in a bracket indicates the source from which the seed was obtained.

Chicago Market (Vick). Plant growth of medium character, spreading, healthy. Tuber with white or pinkish skin, shallow eyes, roundish or short oblong, flattened or round; skin rough. Does not do well here.

Clark's No. 1 (Henderson). Plants make an inferior showing. Tubers white, smooth skinned, usually rather long, eyes quite shallow. Does not do well here.

Crown Queen (Everitt). A strong grower. Tubers very regular in size, white, exceedingly smooth skin, eyes fairly prominent, oblong, flattened, about twice as long as broad.

Dakota Red (Thorburn). Plants of fair size, strong and healthy. Tuber large, usually more than twice as long as broad, eyes prominent, skin pink or reddish, rather inclined to be prongy; not large. Suffered rather badly from rot. The same variety from Everitt also made a poor showing.

Dakota Seedling (Everitt). Plants strong and vigorous, and fair growers. Tuber resembles a lady finger in form, being three times as long as broad, round; smooth, reddish skin; medium deep eyes. Very regular in size Of not much value.

Dictator (Thorburn). Plants make a large, spreading, flourishing growth. Tuber large, short, oval, rather flattish; white, rough skin; medium deep eyes; square at both ends. Makes a good showing, and is very desirable.

Early Albino (Thorburn). Growth of plants small, straggling, puny. Tuber small, short, roundish oblong, white, shallow eyed, smooth skinned. Yielded poorly, and is not desirable.

Early Gem (Vick). Plants inferior, light green and spreading. Tuber small to medium, white, fairly smooth skinned, eyes few and shallow, flat, round or short flat, oval. Not worthy of culture here.

Early Goodrich (Johnson & Co.) Plants medium growers. Tubers small, long, round, white, deep eyed; seems much disposed to rot. Is not desirable.

Early Market (Vick). A healthy growing variety. Tuber thick, blunt, oval, rough skinned, white, shallow eyed. A large, shapely, desirable tuber.

Early Ohio (Everitt). A large and vigorous growing variety. Tuber dark reddish-blue, rough, prongy, deep eyed, short, oblong, well rounded; average length three inches. A good appearing tuber. The same variety from Henderson produced inferior plants, with tubers similar to the above.

Early Puritan (Henderson). Very inferior plant growth. Tuber white, smooth, shallow eyed, round and regular. Makes a fair showing.

Early Rose (Henderson). Very poor plant growth. Tubers white, smooth, shallow eyed, about three times as long as broad, flattened. rough. Fair.

Early Sunrise (Henderson). Growth small and medium strong. Tuber white, smooth, round or oval, flattened, of regular shape. Averages about the size of a hen's egg. Inferior.

Early Vermont (Landreth). Growth rather inferior. Tuber white, deep eyed, rough. oval, flattened. Average length two inches. Makes a poor display.

Empire State (Henderson). Plants, fine, large, vigorous. Tuber white, smooth, long, irregular, prongy, flattened; three or four times as long as broad. Makes a good showing.

Everitt (Everitt). A very strong, healthy, large grower. Tuber white, smooth, slender, long, oval; about twice as long as broad; shallow eyed. A good potato.

Garfield (Landreth). A large, strong grower. Tuber white, shallow eyed, rough, broadly oblong, irregular . Makes a splendid showing.

General McLean (Wilson). A good average grower, producing plants of fair size. Tuber white, smooth, shallow eyed, irregular in size and shape, often being long and broad. Makes a fair showing.

Great Eastern (Thorburn). A strong, vigorous grower. Tuber white, rough, deep eyed, uneven in size and shape. Makes a good showing.

Green Mountain (Everitt). Strong, large grower. Tuber white skinned, not very smooth, medium deep eyed, slightly flattened, not long, of fair size. The same variety from Vick and Wilson made a fine showing.

Illinois (Everitt). Plants large, luxuriant growers. Tuber large, long, round, reddish shallow eyed. Of fair to good appearance.

June Early (Wilson). Fair grower. Tuber white, smooth, deep eyed, round, oval, uniform in size. Very ordinary. The same variety from Everitt made an excellent showing, and differed from Wilson's seed in being long and irregular.

Late Beauty of Hebron (Thorburn). Large, strong grower. Tuber white, long, round, slim, prongy, shallow eyed; three to five inches long. Fairly productive.

Maine Rose (Wilson). Growth large, strong and healthy. Tuber white, smooth, prongy, large, long, of good appearance.

Mammoth Pearl (Landreth). Growth strong and healthy. Tuber large, broad, oval, rough, white, deep eyed, regular in form. Very desirable,

Mammoth White Chief (Bouk). Medium grower. Tuber white, smooth, deep eyed, large, long, round, sometimes prongy. Makes poor showing.

Mayflower (Thorburn). Growth small but healthy. Tuber rough, white, irregular in size and shape, shallow eyed. Not desirable here.

McFadden's Favorite (Bouk). A large, luxurious growing variety, producing a profusion of foliage. Tuber white, smooth, broad, oval, regular in size and shape. Quite desirable for productiveness.

Morning Star (Thorburn). Extra large and strong grower. Tubers long, white, prongy, shallow eyed, flattened, about three times as long as broad. Desirable.

New Queen (Everitt). A fair growing variety. Tubers reddish, rough, round, long, deep eyed, regular in shape, of good appearance. The same named seed from Bouk produced white, smooth, deep eyed, regular tubers.

North Georgia, Native (Johnson). Plant growth large, healthy, dark green. Tuber large, broad, oval, white, flattened, shallow eyed, of good appearance.

No. 50 Seedling (Vick). A fair grower. Tuber white, smooth, shallow eyed, prongy, irregular in size and shape. Makes a fair showing.

Ohio, Junior (Vick). Plants small, dwarfed and inferior. Tuber very large, white, prongy, irregular in size and shape, deep eyed. Makes a good showing.

O. K. Mammoth Prolific (Thorburn) Growth of plant large and luxurious. Tuber white, flat, oval, shallow eyed, smooth. Average in appearance.

Peachblow Seedling (Bouk). Growth medium, with small and sparse leaves. Tuber smooth, red skinned, large, long, round, deep eyed, regular in size and shape. Very desirable.

Pearl of Savoy (Henderson). Growth small and dwarfed. Tuber white, smooth, oval, flattened, shallow eyed. Very poor showing.

Peerless (Johnson & Co). Inferior, dwarfed growth from part of seed, and strong and healthy from others. Tuber large, white, oval, flattened, shallow eyed. Makes a good showing, and is desirable.

Perfect Peachblow (Henderson). Growth large and luxuriant. Tuber white, smooth, deep eyed, round. An average showing.

Poland (Everitt). Tuber white, smooth, shallow eyed, long, regular, flattened. Of fair appearance.

Potentate (Everitt). Growth large and vigorous. Tuber, white smooth, round, flattened, shallow eyed, regular shape. Makes a fair average appearance.

Prairie Queen (Bouk). Plants rather small of growth. Tuber white, smooth, shallow eyed, irregular in size and shape. Makes a poor showing.

Pride of the Field (Wilson). Growth large, dark green, healthy. Tuber smooth, deep eyed, pink skinned, large, prongy, broad, oval. Of good appearance.

Pride of Nebraska (Bouk). Strong, good grower. Tuber long, round, reddish-blue, especially the eyes, usually regular in size and shape, deep eyed. Rather poor.

Prince Edward Island Rose (Landreth). Growth small, dwarfed and unhealthy. Tuber white, smooth, shallow eyed, egg shaped. Inferior variety.

Rose's Beauty of Beauties (Bouk). Growth unhealthy and small. Tuber white, smooth, shallow eyed, long, slender, averaging very small. Very inferior.

Rose's Beauty of Hebron (Thorburn). Growth large, luxuriant and strong. Tuber does not resemble the Beauty of Hebron. Form inclines to round or short oblong, eyes fairly prominent. skin rough, white. Yields evenly. Makes a good showing in the field.

Rose's New Giant (Thorburn). Tuber white, smooth, long, large, irregular, deep eyed, prongy. Four or five times as long as broad. Quite desirable.

Rose's Seedling (Wilson). A good growing variety. Tuber white, smooth, deep eyed, very large, broad, oval. Makes good average showing.

Rural Blush (Henderson). Tuber white, rough, deep eyed, long, somewhat prongy, very large. Excellent.

Rural New Yorker No. 2 (Henderson). Tuber white, smooth, shallow eyed, very large, irregular. Desirable.

Snowflake (Johnson & Co). Tuber white, smooth, oval, flat, shallow eyed. Of good appearance.

Snow Queen (Thorburn). Tuber white, smooth, shallow eyed, egg shaped, less than a goose egg in size. Not very productive.

State of Maine (Wilson). Growth large, strong, thrifty. Tuber white, smooth, shallow eyed, oval, flat, very large. Prolific and quite desirable.

Stray Beauty (Wilson). Growth small, low, dwarfed. Tuber smooth, red skinned, spherical, regular in size and shape, shallow eyed. A fair average variety.

Sunlit Star (Thorburn). Growth fair. Tuber white, smooth, shallow eyed, irregular, averaging small. Makes a poor showing.

Thorburn (Thorburn). Growth small and inferior. Tuber white, smooth, shallow eyed, irregular in size and shape. A poor producer.

Thorburn's Late Rose (Thorburn). Growth, large, healthy, vigorous. Tuber white, smooth, deep eyed, sometimes prongy, long, irregular Makes a fair showing.

Triumph (Henderson). Growth small and very inferior. Tuber white, smooth, globular, small. Unproductive and undesirable.

Vanguard (Henderson). Growth small and dwarfed. Tuber smooth, white skinned, egg shaped in form and size, shallow eyed. Inferior.

Vick's Prize (Vick). Growth of plants small and dwarfed from single eyes, and of fair size when from whole tubers. Tubers rough, irregular, white, deep eyed. Of good appearance.

Watson's Seedling (Wilson). A fair grower. Tuber smooth, white long, round, sometimes prongy, shallow eyed. Makes a good showing.

White Elephant (Johnson & Co.) Plant growth large, dark green, luxurious. Tuber white, smooth, shallow eyed, long, large, sometimes prongy. Desirable. Seed of this same name from Thorburn produced large, white, rough, prongy, shallow eyed, fine tubers.

White Star (Henderson). Growth very large and flourishing. Tuber white, smooth, sometimes prongy, long, round, very large shallow eyed. Very desirable, and of fine appearance.

White Superior (Vick). Growth healthy, strong. Tuber white, smooth, deep eyed, oval, flat, large, sometimes prongy, regular in size and shape. Of good average appearance.

Among the above the following are especially to be recommended: American Giant, Boley's Northern Spy, Burbank, Dictator, Early Market, Garfield, Mammoth Pearl, Peachblow Seedling, Peerless, Rural Blush, State of Maine, White Elephant and White Star.

COMPARISON OF KEEPING QUALITIES.

After digging the above varieties, one sample hill of each was placed in a paper sack, and carried to a building where the atmosphere was dry and not subject to great fluctuation, and no fire existed. Each sack was closed and laid on the floor, with nothing over it. These potatoes remained here till February 14, when an examination was made of their condition, which is herewith given. Those that were flabby and soft are in one column, and those firm and hard of flesh in another.

Flabby.	*Firm.*

Flabby.

Bliss's Triumph. not badly sprouted.
Boston Market, slightly sp'ted.
Charles Downing,   "   "
Chicago Market, badly   "
Crown Queen, not   "   "
Early Albino, "   "   "
  "   Gem, - badly   "
  "   Goodrich, slightly   "
  "   Market,   "   "
  "   Puritan, •   "   "
  "   Rose, -   "   "
  "   Sunrise, badly   "
  "   Vermont,   "   "
Gen McLean -   "   "
Great Eastern, somewhat   "
June Early, very little   "
Mammoth Pearl, badly   "
Mammoth White Chief, some-what sprouted.
Mayflower, not much sprouted
Ohio Junior, somewhat   "
Pearl of Savoy, little   "
Prairie Queen - badly   "
P. E. Island Rose, not badly sprouted.
Rose's Beauty of Beauties, some-what sprouted.
State of Maine, somew't sprout'd.
Stray Beauty,   "   "
Triumph -   "   "
Vanguard. very little   "
Vick's Prize, considerably   "
White Superior, badly   "

Firm.

Beauty of Hebron, sprouted but little.
Boley's Northern Spy, hardly no sprouts.
Burbank, - badly sprouted.
Clark's No. 1   "   "
Dakota Red. very little   "
Dakota Seedling, ver. litt. "
Dictator. - very little   "
Early Ohio - badly   "
Empire State, somewhat   "
Garfield, - badly   "
Green Mountain. somewh't "
Late Beauty of Hebron, little sprouted.
McFadden's Favorite, rather badly sprouted.
Morning Star, rather badly sp'd.
New Queen, very badly sprout'd.
New Zealand, somewhat   "
North Ga. Native, badly   "
No. 50 Seedling, badly   "
O. K Mammoth Prolific, badly sprouted.
Peachblow Seedl'g, sligh'y sp'd.
Peerless, somewhat sprouted
Perfect Peachblow, little   "
Poland - rather   "
Potentate, very badly   "
Pride of the Field,   "   "
Pride of Neb., very   "   "
Rose's B'ty of Heb'n, sl'tly "
Rose's Seedling, v'y. sl'tly "
Rose's New Giant, badly   "
Rural Blush, not badly   "
Snowflake - badly   "
Snow Queen -   "   "
Thorburn - little   "
Thorburn's Late Rose, not badly sprouted.
Watson's Seedling. not badly sprouted.
White Elephant. badly sprouted.
White Star, not badly   "

DEVELOPMENTAL STAGES OF VARIETIES OF POTATOES.

		Planted.	Vegetated	Bloomed	Ripe	No. of days from plant'g to ripen'g
1	American Giant	April 22	May 5	....	July 12	81
2	Beauty of Hebron	March 12	March 30	May 15	" 22	132
3	Bliss's Triumph	April 22	May 5	....	" 12	81
4	Boley's Northern Spy	March 16	April 10	May 15	" 26	132
5	Boston Market	" 12	" 3	...	June 27	107
6	Burbank	" 12	" 11	June 29	July 28	138
7	California Peachblow	April 22	May 7	....	" 12	81
8	Charles Downing	March 12	April 3	....	June 27	107
9	Charter Oak	" 12	" 3	....	July 12	122
10	Chicago Market	" 12	" 3	May 28	" 12	122
11	Clark' No. 1	" 12	" 3	" 20	June 29	109
12	Crown Queen	April 22	May 5	June 6	July 3	71
13	Dakota Red	March 12	April 11	" 13	" 28	137
14	Dakota Seedling	April 22	May 7	" 25	......	....
15	Dictator ....,..	March 12	April 5	May 13	July 24	133
16	Early Albino	" 12	" 3	. ....	June 27	107
17	" Gem	" 12	" 3	May 20	" 30	110
18	" Goodrich	" 12	" 9	" 13	" 30	110
19	" Market	" 12	" 13	....	July 12	122
20	" Ohio	" 12	" 8	....	June 30	110
21	" Rose	" 12	" 2	May 13	" 30	110
22	" Sunrise	" 12	" 3	" 15	July 10	120
23	" Puritan	" 12	" 3	.... ..	June 26	106
24	" Vermont	" 12	" 3	....	" 25	105
25	Empire State	" 12	" 5	May 9	July 20	130
26	Garfield	" 12	" 8	" 13	" 12	122
27	Everitt	April 22	May 5	June 10	" 12	81
28	Gen. McLean	March 16	April 3	. ...	" 26	132
29	Great Eastern	" 12	" 3	May 28	" 17	127
30	Green Mountain	" 12	" 3	" 30	" 15	125
31	Illinois	" 12	" 10	" 12	" 24	134
32	June Early	April 22	May 5	June 6	" 1	70
33	Late Beauty of Hebron	March 12	April 10	May 12	" 24	134
34	Maine Rose	" 16	" 8	" 19	" 24	130
35	Mammoth Pearl	" 12	" 5	....	" 15	125
36	Mammoth White Chief	" 16	" 18	....	Aug. 2	139
37	Mayflower......	" 12	" 5	June 9	....	
38	McFadden's Favorite	" 16	" 8	....	July 22	128
39	Morning Star	" 12	" 5	May 12	" 24	134
40	New Queen	" 16	" 10	" 20	" 1	107
41	North Georgia Native.	" 12	" 5	......	" 17	127
42	No. 50 Seedling	" 12	" 5	May 20	" 7	117
43	Ohio Junior	" 12	" 10	....	June 25	105
44	O. K. Mam'th Prolific	" 12	" 8	May 12	July 15	125
45	Peachblow Seeding ..	" 16	" 5	....	" 12	118
46	Pearl of Savoy	" 12	" 3	....	June 23	103
47	Peerless	" 12	" 3	....	" 21	101
48	Perfect Peachblow ..	" 12	" 8	June 9	July 9	119
49	Poland	April 22	May 5	" 4	" 10	78

DEVELOPMENTAL STAGES—CONTINUED.

		Planted	Vegetated	Bloomed	Ripe	No. of days from plant'g to ripen'g
50	Potentate	April 22	May 5	June 17	July 15	84
51	Prairie Queen	March 16	April 12	.. ....	" 12	118
52	Pride of Nebraska....	" 16	" 15	May 27	" 15	121
53	Pride of the Field	" 16	" 10	" 8	" 15	121
54	Prince Ed. Isl'nd Rose	" 12	" 5	....	June 25	105
55	Rose's B'ty of B'ties .	" 16	" 10	....	July 12	118
56	Rose's B'ty of Hebron	" 12	" 3	June 14	" 24	134
57	Rose's New Giant ...	" 12	" 8	May 30	" 10	120
58	Rose's Seedling .	" 16	" 5	" 12	" 26	132
59	Rural Blush	" 12	" 9	" 19	" 22	132
60	Rural N. Yorker No. 2	" 12	" 9	June 5	" 17	127
61	Snowflake	" 12	" 3	....	" 15	125
62	Snow Queen	" 12	" 3	......	" 10	120
63	State of Maine	" 12	" 3	June 20	" 15	125
64	Stray Beauty	" 16	" 10	. .	June 12	57
65	Sunlit Star	" 12	" 13	" 20	July 12	122
66	Triumph	" 12	" 3	. . .	June 25	105
67	Thorburn	" 12	" 3	....	" 25	105
68	Thorburn's Late Rose	" 12	" 3	June 17	July 28	138
69	Vanguard	" 12	" 3	....	June 20	100
70	Vick's Prize	" 12	" 3	....	July 4	114
71	Watson's Seedling	" 16	" 5	May 13	" 24	132
72	White Elephant......	" 12	" 9	June 24	" 26	136
73	" Star	" 12	" 9	June 1	August 2	143
74	" Superior	" 12	" 8	" 12	July 26	136

Five of Shortest Period of Growth.

Stray Beauty........ .	57 days
June Early	70 "
Crown Queen·	71 "
Poland	78 "
American Giant ....⎫	
Bliss's Triumph ....⎬ 81 "	
Everitt ....⎪	
California Peachblow ....⎭	

Five of Longest Period of Growth.

White Star	143 days
Mammoth White Chief ..	139 "
Thorburn's Late Rose ..	138 "
Burbank	138 "
Dakota Red	137 "

(d.) Early vs. Late Culture for Sweet Potatoes.

Six plats, each one-twentieth of an acre in size, were planted to sweet potatoes at weekly intervals. The land is a light clay-loam and fairly level. During the years 1887 and 1888 red clover was grown upon it. The rows extended north and south, were four feet apart with the plants 14 inches apart in the rows The Southern Queen variety of sweet potato was grown. The soil was very thoroughly plowed and harrowed, being given extra tillage. The culture was flat. From the beginning the plant growth was most excellent. No fertilizer was used. Tillage was as frequent as was necessary, all plats receiving like treatment.

24

Agricultural Library

The following table shows the results of planting:

TABLE IX.

YIELDS OF SWEET POTATOES PLANTED AT DIFFERENT DATES.

Date Planted	YIELD		Total Crop
	Merchantable	Unmerchantable	
April 27............	363 lbs.	118 lbs.	481 lbs.
May 4..............	507 "	138 "	645 "
" 11.............	261 "	80½ "	341½ "
" 18	249 "	67½ "	316½ "
" 25..............	523½ "	76 "	599½ "
June 1	534 "	82 "	616½ "

One cannot draw absolute conclusions from the above table, yet the following facts should not be overlooked:

(1) The largest yield was produced from the planting of May 4th.

(2) Many more unmerchantable potatoes were produced from the first three than from the last three plantings.

(3) The average yield for the first three plats, or *early planted*, is 489 pounds; of the *late planted*, or last three plats, 510 pounds, or a difference of 21 pounds in favor of later planting.

(4) The average yield of the plantings from April 27th to May 11th was smaller than those planted from May 18th to June 1st, and each plat contained on an average 37 pounds more of unmerchantable tubers than did the several late plantings.

In conclusion, I wish to here express my special indebtedness to Mr. W. N. Price, a junior student in the University of Tennessee, who, under my direction, was largely intrusted with the field work in connection with the data reported in this Bulletin.

Lightning Source UK Ltd.
Milton Keynes UK
UKHW050644150421
382040UK00008B/681